2ND EDITION
**WORKBOOK**

# Contents

# 1 In My Classroom

## Vocabulary

**1**  **Listen and number.**

**2** **Look at 1. Write.**

| cutting | gluing | listening | ~~coloring~~ | using | writing |

**1** They're ____coloring____ the picture.

**2** She's _____ her name.

**3** They're _____ to a story.

**4** She's _____ shapes.

**5** He's _____ the computer.

**6** He's _____ shapes.

**How did I do?** ☆ ☆ ☆

**3** **Listen and sing. Then match and write.**

**a**

_____

**b**

Peter

## Here's My Classroom!

Look! Here's my classroom.
And here are my friends!
Peter, Sarah, and Timothy,
Penny, Jack, and Jen!

Peter is cutting paper.
Penny is writing her name.
Sarah is listening to a story,
And Jack is playing a game.

Timothy is counting.
Jen is gluing.
We have fun and learn a lot.
What are your friends doing?

**c**

_____

**d**

_____

**4** **Draw your classroom. Then say.**

**5** **Read and write.**

## What's Maria Doing?

1 How many Marias are there in the class?

There are _____ Marias.

2 What is one Maria doing?

She's _____ and

_____.

3 What is the other Maria doing?

She's _____.

---

**THINK BIG**

**What do you like doing? Read and circle.**

using the computer        writing        reading
listening        cutting        gluing
watching a movie        playing a game

---

**How did I do?**   ☆ ☆ ☆

**6** **Look and match. Then say.**

**1** What's she doing?

She's listening to a story.

**a**

**2** What are they doing?

They're watching a movie.

**b**

**3** What's he doing?

He's gluing shapes.

**c**

**7** **Find the words. Circle.**

| coloring | counting | ~~cutting~~ | gluing |
|---|---|---|---|
| listening | playing | using | writing |

| e | s | d | x | d | g | d | v | m | c |
|---|---|---|---|---|---|---|---|---|---|
| m | i | n | g | i | l | u | r | e | o |
| n | g | a | t | f | a | s | g | k | u |
| g | o | p | l | a | y | i | n | g | n |
| c | o | l | o | r | i | n | g | e | t |
| u | n | g | t | u | n | g | l | d | i |
| t | g | o | i | f | g | a | u | g | n |
| t | l | i | s | t | e | n | i | n | g |
| i | s | w | r | i | t | i | n | g | a |
| n | p | a | e | n | t | t | g | i | t |
| g | i | f | o | i | a | s | f | n | o |

# Grammar

| What's he/she **doing**? | He's /She's **reading** a book. |
| What **are** they **doing**? | They're **gluing** pictures. |

**8** **Look and write.**

| are they (x2) | He's (x2) | She's | They're (x2) | What's he (x2) | What's she |

**1** What _____ doing? _____ listening.

**2** _____ doing? _____ cutting.

**3** _____ doing? _____ coloring.

**4** What _____ doing? _____ playing a game.

**5** _____ doing? _____ counting.

**How did I do?**  ☆ ☆ ☆

**9** **Look and match.**

1  2  3  4

**a** gluing  **b** playing  **c** reading  **d** writing

**10** **Look at 9. Write the answers.**

**1** What are they doing?  They _____ a book.

**2** What's he doing?  He _____ shapes.

**3** What's she doing?  She _____ numbers.

**4** What are they doing?  They _____ soccer.

| How many pictures are there? | **There's** one picture. |
|---|---|
| How many books are there? | **There are** three books. |

**11** **Look at 8. Read and ✓.**

**1** There are ☐ one ball. ☐ four backpacks.

**2** There's ☐ one ball. ☐ four backpacks.

**12** **Write the words and the number.**

| equals (x2) | minus | plus |

**1**

6 pencils _____ 6 pencils _____ ☐ pencils

**2**

10 soccer balls _____ 5 soccer balls _____ ☐ soccer balls

**13** **Listen and read. Write + or –, =, and the number.**

**1**

14 apples    minus    8 apples    equals    ☐ apples.

**2**

10 markers    plus    2 markers    equals    ☐ markers.

**3**

6 shapes    plus    8 shapes    equals    ☐ shapes.

**How did I do?** ☆☆☆

**14** **Find and circle** th.

| ss | f | t | wh |
|---|---|---|---|
| v | ff | th | w |
| zz | h | ch | z |

**15** **Read and circle** th.

**1** bath **2** path **3** this **4** that

**16** **Match the words with the same sounds.**

**1** they      **a** thin
**2** math      **b** then

**27**
**17** **Listen and chant.**

There are three crocodiles
Taking a bath.
They have thin mouths,
But big teeth!
Look out! Look out!

**18**  **Read and match. Then say.**

**a**

**1** May I use the markers now?

**b**

**2** Yes. Sit down, Mark. It's your turn.

**c**

**3** It's fun taking turns!

**19**  **Read and write.**

| fun | Let's | May | now |

**Anita:** _____ I use the computer _____?

**Sam:** Yes! _____ take turns.

**Anita:** OK. It's _____ taking turns!

**How did I do?**  ☆ ☆ ☆

**20**  **Look and write. Use the correct form of the verb.**

| draw | play | sing | use |

**1** What's she doing?

She's _____ a song.

**2** What are they doing?

They're _____ a game.

**3** What's he doing?

He's _____ on the board.

**4** What are they doing?

They're _____ computers.

**21**  **Count and write. Use is or are.**

| Our Classroom | |
|---|---|
| computer | I |
| chairs | IIIII IIIII IIIII III |
| boys | IIIII III |
| girls | IIIII IIII |
| teacher | I |

**1** There _____is 1_____ computer.

**2** There _____ chairs.

**3** There _____ boys.

**4** There _____ girls.

**5** There _____ teacher.

# 2 My Games

## Vocabulary

**1** **Read and match. Then say.**

**1** kick a soccer ball

**2** play basketball

**3** skate

**4** skateboard

**5** ride a bike

**6** play on the slide

a

b

c

d

e

f

How did I do? ☆☆☆

# Song

**2** **Listen and sing. Then match.**

a

b

## Come On and Play

We're playing on the playground.
There are lots of games to play.
Soccer, baseball, and basketball.
What do you want to play today?

Paul likes to play on the swings.
Vera likes to play on the slide.
We all like to play hide-and-seek.
Are you ready to run and hide?

We're playing on the playground.
It's always so much fun.
Come on and play with us.
We play with everyone!

d

c

e

**3** **Draw. Then say.**

**My Games**

**4** **Read and write.**

# We Like to Play Together!

1 What does Jamie like to do?

He likes _____.

2 What does Jenny like to do?

She likes _____.

3 What does Tony like to do?

He likes _____.

4 What do they all like to do?

They like _____.

**THINK BIG** Circle the odd one out.

How did I do? ☆☆☆

**5** **Follow the path. Count and write.**

ten + ten + ten + ten
= fourty balls

= 10 balls

**1** _fourty balls_

**2** _____

**3** _____

**4** _____

**5** _____

**6** _____

**6** **Look at 5. What do they like to do? Write.**

| jump | ~~play baseball~~ | ride her bike | skate | skateboard |

**1** They like to ___play baseball___.

**2** He likes to _____.

**3** She likes to _____.

**4** They like to _____.

**5** She likes to _____.

| | |
|---|---|
| What **does** he/she **like to do**? | He/She **likes to skate**. |
| What **do** they **like to do**? | They **like to play basketball**. |

**7** **Write do or does. Then listen and match.**

**1** What _____

he like to do?

a

**2** What _____

they like to do?

b

**3** What _____

she like to do?

c

**4** What _____

they like to do?

d

**8** **Look at 7. Write the answers.**

**1** He _____ ride his bike.

**2** They _____ skate.

**3** She _____ read.

**4** They _____ play hide-and-seek.

How did I do? ☆ ☆ ☆

**9** **Look and write.**

| behind | between | in front of | next to |

Where are they?

**1** Dan is _____ Julia.

**2** Amy is _____ Zach and Mark.

**3** Tess is _____ Pat.

**4** Pat is _____ Tess.

**10** **Look at 5. Read and circle.**

**1** Pat likes to **skate** / **skateboard**.

**2** Amy likes to play **soccer** / **basketball**.

**3** Zach and Dan like to play **soccer** / **baseball**.

**4** Julia likes to **jump** / **ride her bike**.

**11** **Look and write.**

bone   foot
hand   muscle

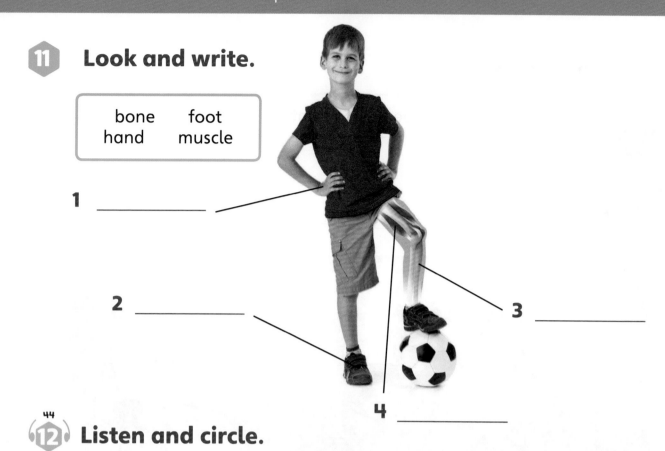

1 _____

2 _____

3 _____

4 _____

44
**12** **Listen and circle.**

1
3   13
30  34

2
7   27
37  72

3
7   17
70  77

4
6   16
26  62

How did I do?   ☆ ☆ ☆

**13** **Find and circle ng and nk.**

n    m    nk    l

g    k    t    ck

gg    ng    mm    h

**14** **Read and circle ng and nk.**

**1** ring    **2** pink    **3** bang    **4** ink

**15** **Match the words with the same sounds.**

**1** wing    **a** sink

**2** bank    **b** sing

**16** **Listen and chant.**
50

Sing a song about a king.
Thank you! Thank you!
He has a big, pink ring
And big, blue wings.
Thank you! Thank you!

**How did I do?** ☆ ☆ ☆

**17** **Read and match.**

**1**

Always wear a helmet and knee pads.

**a**

**2**

Always put one leg on each side.

**b**

**3**

Always sit down.

**c**

**4**

Always keep your feet in front of you.

**d**

How did I do?

**18** **Look and write. Where is Milo?**

| behind     between |
| in front of    next to |

1 _____

2 _____

3 _____

4 _____

**52**
**19** **Listen and match. Then write.**

Mario  Terry

Sarah  Pete

**1** What does Terry like to do? She likes _____.

**2** What does Pete like to do? He likes _____.

**3** What does Sarah like to do? She likes _____.

**4** What does Mario like to do? He likes _____.

**How did I do?** ☆☆☆

# 3 In My House

## Vocabulary

**1** **Look and write. Then match.**

bathroom
bedroom
kitchen
living room

bed
chair
closet
couch
dresser
fridge
table
TV

**2** **Look at 1. What's in the rooms? Write.**

**1** There's a _____, a _____, and a _____
in the bedroom.

**2** There's a _____, a _____, and a _____
in the kitchen.

How did I do?   ☆ ☆ ☆

# Song

 **58**

**3** **Listen and sing. Circle the pictures from the song.**

## Where Are My Keys?

**1** Where are my keys, Mom?
Your keys are on the chair.
The chair? Which chair?
There are chairs everywhere!

**2** There's a chair in the living room
And one in the bedroom, too.
There are chairs in the dining room.
I don't know which chair. Do you?

**3** Your keys are where you left them.
Put on your glasses and see.
They're on the chair behind you.
My keys are there! Silly me!

a  b

a  b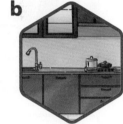

a  b

**4** **Look in your house. Count and write the number.**

**1** There are _____ chairs in the living room.

**2** There are _____ chairs in the bedroom.

**3** There are _____ chairs in the kitchen.

**4** There are _____ chairs in the dining room.

**How did I do?** ☆ ☆ ☆

**5** **Read and circle.**

## A family visit

These are my cousins. They're my aunt and uncle's children.

Where are your cousins now?

They're in the kitchen. Look!

Jamie, where's the TV?

It's in the living room.

1 The boys are Jamie's **brothers** / **cousins**.

2 The boys' mother is Jamie's **aunt** / **uncle**.

3 The boys are in the **bedroom** / **kitchen**.

4 The TV is in the **kitchen** / **living room**.

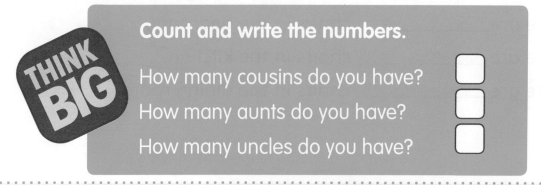

THINK BIG

**Count and write the numbers.**

How many cousins do you have? ☐

How many aunts do you have? ☐

How many uncles do you have? ☐

How did I do? ☆☆☆

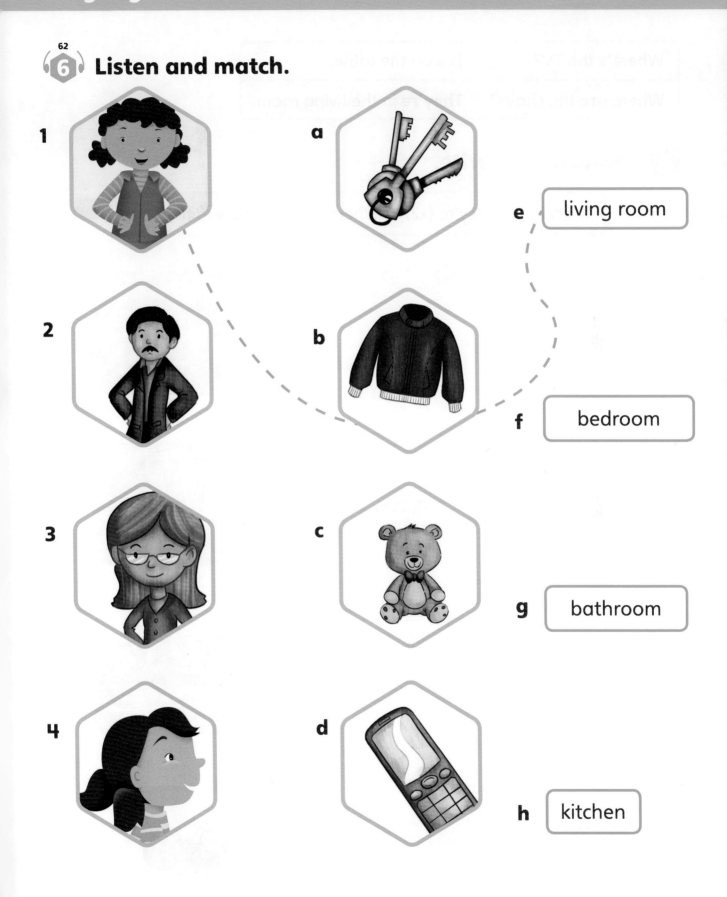

**6** **Listen and match.**

1

2

3

4

a

b

c

d

e living room

f bedroom

g bathroom

h kitchen

# Grammar

| Where**'s** the TV? | **It's** on the table. |
|---|---|
| Where **are** the chairs? | **They're** in the living room. |

**7** **Follow and write.**

> It's (x2)    They're (x2)    Where's (x2)    Where are (x2)

**1** ___Where's___ the table?
___It's___ next to
the couch.

 **a**

**2** _____ my keys?
_____ behind
the chair.

 **b**

**3** _____ his shoes?
_____ on the chair.

**c**

**4** _____ the oven?
_____ next to
the sink.

 **d**

How did I do?  ☆ ☆ ☆

My mother**'s** phone is on the dresser.

Ben**'s** keys are on the table.

**8** **Look and write. Use 's.**

**1** Dan →

They're _____ glasses.

**2** Suzie →

It's _____ phone.

**3** my mom →

It's _____ computer.

**4** her brother →

It's _____ bike.

**9** **Read the puzzles. Look at 8. Then write.**

**1** It's behind the table, next to the chair. What is it?

It's her brother's bike.

**2** It's on the table, between the lamp and the bike. What is it?

_____

**3** They're on the chair behind the kite. What are they?

_____

**4** It's on the dressing table, next to the backpack. What is it?

_____

**How did I do?** ☆ ☆ ☆

**10** **Write the names of the objects. Then write old or new.**

| bike | computer | fridge | lamp | phone | TV |

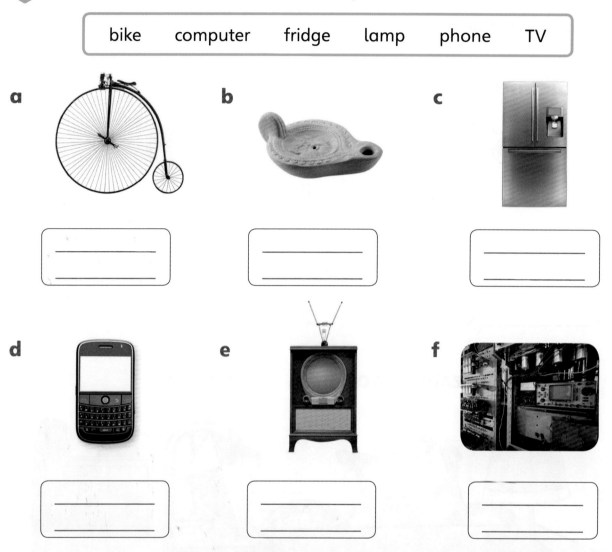

**a**

**b**

**c**

**d**

**e**

**f**

**64**

**11** **Listen and read. Match with the old objects in 10.**

**1** It's nearly 2,000 years old. It needs oil in it. The oil burns.

**2** Today we put them in our backpacks. But you can't put this one in your backpack. It needs a big room!

**3** It's very big, but the screen is very small.

**4** It has two wheels – a big wheel and a small wheel.
When you ride it, you sit on the big wheel. It's fun!

How did I do? ☆☆☆

**12**  **Find and circle oo.**

a    o    ee    u

oo    i    oa    ue

oe    ow    ou    ea

**13**  **Read and circle oo.**

**1** moon    **2** book    **3** zoo    **4** foot

**14**  **Match the words with the same sounds.**

**1** food      **a** look

**2** good      **b** cool

**15**  **Listen and chant.**

Look in my cookbook.
The food is good!
The food is cool!

How did I do? ☆☆☆

**72**

**16** **Listen and number. Then say.**

**a**

I put my dirty dishes in the sink.

**b**

I put my dirty clothes in the washing machine.

**c**

I put my toys in the toy box.

**17** **Look at 16. Find and write the words.**

1 _____   xbo  yot

2 _____   niks

3 _____   ngihsaw  hcamein

**18** **How do you keep your bedroom neat? Draw and write.**

I _____.

**How did I do?** ☆☆☆

# Review

**19** **Look and write.**

| bathtub | bed | chair | couch | fridge | lamp | oven | sink |

1 _____

2 _____

3 _____

4 _____

5 _____

6 _____

7 _____

8 _____

**20** **Look at 19. Match.**

**1** Where's the oven?     **a** They're in the dining room.

**2** Where's the bathtub?     **b** It's in the kitchen next to the sink.

**3** Where are the chairs?     **c** It's in the bathroom.

**21** **Look at 19. Write.**

**1** What's in the kitchen?
There's a _____ and an _____.

**2** What's in the bathroom?
There's a _____ and a _____.

**1    Look, find, and number.** 🔍  🔍 **MY CLASSROOM**

**1** cutting paper
**2** gluing shapes
**3** using a computer

**2** **Read and find. Circle the activities in the picture.**

**At your school:**

What do you do on the playground and in the classroom?

**In your house:**

What do you have in your bedroom?

**3** **Think big, look, and draw.**

One thing is in the bedroom, in the classroom, and on the playground. What is it?

**4** **In Your Classroom**

Work in groups and share.

## MY GAMES

4 play on the seesaw
5 play on the slide
6 play on the swings

## MY HOUSE

7 a bed
8 a closet
9 a lamp

## Vocabulary

**1** **Look and match.**

**1** train station

a

**2** movie theater

b

c

**3** bank

d

**4** restaurant

e

**5** supermarket

How did I do? ☆☆☆

**80**
 **2** **Listen and sing. Circle the places on the map.**

## Maps Are Great!

Where's the bookstore?
I want to buy a book.
Here, I have a map.
Come on. Let's take a look!

The bookstore is on River Street.
It isn't far from us.
Do you want to walk there?
No, thanks! Let's take the bus!

I want to mail a letter, too.
Is there a post office, do you know?
I'm looking at the map. Yes, there is.
It's near the bookstore. Come on. Let's go.

Maps are really great.
I use them every day.
In town or out of town,
They help me find my way!

River Street

Maple Street
Bookstore
Train Station
Post Office
Main Street
Park Street
Music Store
Computer Store
Restaurant
Bus
Elm Street

**3** **What's in your town? Check (✓).**

☐ bookstore          ☐ post office          ☐ bus stop

☐ gas station          ☐ computer store

## 4 Read and ✓.

## Is There a Bookstore?

What kind of shops are there?

1 There's a bookstore.

2 There's a movie theater.

3 There's a computer store.

4 There are restaurants.

5 There are supermarkets.

**What is there in your town? Read and circle.**

bank    supermarket    movie theater
restaurant    train station

**How did I do?** ☆ ☆ ☆

**84**
**5** **Listen and follow the path.**

**6** **Look at 5. Write.**

**Where do they go?**

1 _____post office_____    3 _____    5 _____

2 _____    4 _____

# Grammar

I/We/They/You **want to** mail a letter.  He/She **wants to** go to the park.

**7** **Look and write** want to **or** wants to**.**

me          Amy          Lisa          my brother

**1** I _____ eat pizza.

**3** Lisa _____ buy a computer.

**2** Amy _____ go to the supermarket.

**4** My brother _____ mail a letter.

**8** **Write.**

the bookstore, the movie theater

the gas station, the bank

I want to go _____ _____. I _____ _____.

Mom wants to _____ _____. She _____ _____.

**How did I do?** ☆ ☆ ☆

| | |
|---|---|
| **Is there** a post office near here? | Yes, **there is**. |
| **Is there** a bank on Elm Street? | No, **there isn't**. |

**9** **Draw. Add a post office and a bookstore.**

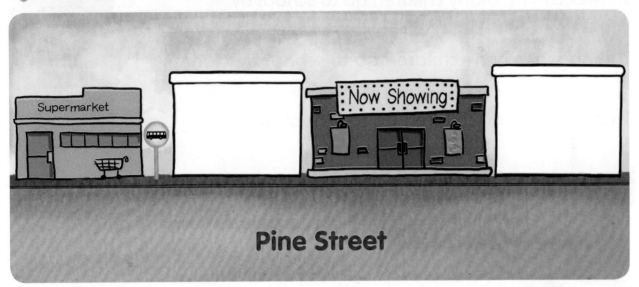

Supermarket

Now Showing

**Pine Street**

**10** **Look at 9. Write Yes, there is or No, there isn't.**

**1** Is there a bus stop on Pine Street?
Yes, there is _____.

**2** Is there a train station on Pine Street?
_____.

**3** Is there a supermarket next to the post office?
_____.

**4** Is there a movie theater between the post office and the bookstore?
_____.

**5** Is there a gas station near the bus stop?
_____.

**11** **Look, read, and write.**

| bike | boat | bus | train |

**1** In London, some children go to school by _____.

**2** In Mexico City, many children go to school by _____.

**3** In Bangkok, many children go to school by _____.

**4** In Beijing, many children go to school by _____.

**12** **Listen, read, and write.** [86]

| bike | canals | fast | ground | without |

There are a lot of [1]_____ in Bangkok. Sunan goes to school by boat.

Lars and his friends live in Amsterdam. They go to school by [2]_____, on bike streets. Bike streets are safe streets [3]_____ cars.

In Mexico City, there a lot of cars on the street. Carmen goes to school by bus because it's [4]_____. Her school is near a bus stop.

Sophia goes to school under the [5]_____. There are 468 subway stations in New York! Sophia's apartment is near a station.

**How did I do?** ☆ ☆ ☆

**13** **Find and circle** ai **and** oa.

i    oo    a    ou

ai    au    oe    o

eu    oa    ie    oi

**14** **Read and circle** ai **and** oa.

**1** [ rain ]    **2** [ coat ]    **3** [ train ]    **4** [ boat ]

**15** **Match the words with the same sounds.**

**1** road        **a** wait

**2** tail         **b** soap

**16** **92** **Listen and write** ai **and** oa. **Then chant.**

Wear a **1**c_____t

To **2**s_____ l the **3**b_____t!

Drive the **4**tr_____n

In the **5**r_____n!

### 17 Read, look, and circle.

a

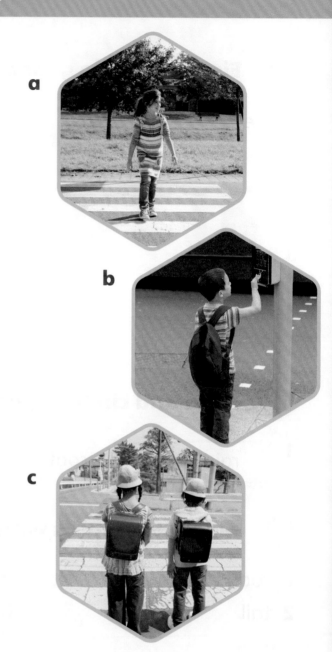

1 I **look** / **don't look** left, then right, then left again before I cross the street.

b

2 I wait for the **blue** / **green** man.

c

3 I **always** / **never** cross at the crosswalk.

### 18 Find and write the words.

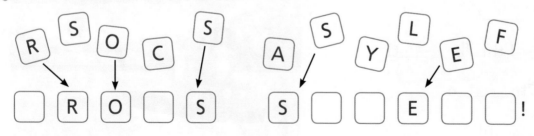

How did I do? ☆ ☆ ☆

# Review

**19** **Write** want to **or** wants to. **Then match.**

1 We _____ buy fruit.

2 She _____ go by train.

3 You _____ go to the bookstore.

4 He _____ buy gas.

**a** There's a bookstore behind the supermarket.

**b** There's a gas station near Park Street.

**c** There's a supermarket on Elm Road.

**d** There's a train station on London Road.

**20** **Read, look, and circle.**

1 In Mexico City, many children go to school by **bus** / **boat**.

2 In Beijing, many children go to school by **train** / **bike**.

3 In London, many children go to school by **boat** / **train**.

4 In Bangkok, many children go to school by **boat** / **bike**.

**21** **Look at** 19. **Write** Yes, there is **or** No, there isn't.

1 Is there a supermarket on Park Street?

_____

2 Is there a train station on London Road?

_____

# My Dream Job

## Vocabulary

**1** Find, circle, and match.

pilot

artist

| a | p | e | o | c | k | a |
|---|---|---|---|---|---|---|
| d | s | i | n | g | e | r |
| o | p | b | l | d | w | t |
| c | i | v | r | o | t | i |
| t | s | i | e | d | t | s |
| o | v | p | r | t | s | t |
| r | h | a | c | t | o | r |

vet

doctor

actor

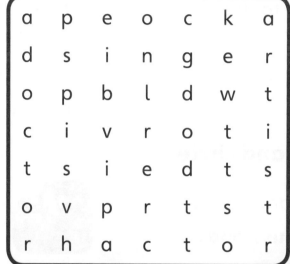

singer

**2** Look and circle.

**1 chef / writer**

**2 athlete / dancer**

How did I do?

# Song

pilot

teacher

## Hey, What Do You Want to Be?

Hey, what do you want to be?
You have to choose just one.
There are so many different jobs.
I want one that is fun!

I want to be a ¹_____
And an athlete, too.
Or maybe a ²_____ .
What about you?

I want to be an ³_____ ,
And I want to be a vet.
I want to be a ⁴_____ , too.
Then I can fly a jet!

**Chorus**

actor

dancer

**4** **Write and draw.**

I want to be **a / an**

_____ .

**5** **Read and circle.**

# Dream Jobs!

What do you want to be, Jenny?

I want to be a singer. I like to sing.

What do you want to be, Dan?

I want to be a writer. I like to write stories.

**1** Jenny wants to be a **singer** / **writer**.

**2** Dan wants to be a **writer** / **singer**.

**3** Jenny and Dan are talking to their **friend** / **teacher**.

**6** **Read the story again. What do they like to do? Match.**

**1** eat

**2** dance

**3** sing

**4** write

a

b

c

d

THINK BIG

Read and circle. I like music. I want to be a _____ and a _____ .

chef     dancer     singer     writer

How did I do?   ☆ ☆ ☆

**7** **Read and write.**

to draw    to fly    to sing    to write

1  What do you want to be?    I want to be a singer. I like _____.

2  What do you want to be?    I want to be an artist. I like _____.

3  What do you want to be?    I want to be a pilot. I like _____.

4  What do you want to be?    I want to be a writer. I like _____.

**8** **What do you like to do? Write and draw.**

I like _____

_____.

# Grammar

| | |
|---|---|
| What **do** you **want to be**? | I **want to be** an actor. |
| What **does** he/she **want to be**? | He/She **wants to be** a doctor. |

**9** **Look, match, and write.**

**1** What do you want to be?

**2** What _____ you _____?　

**3** What _____?　

**4** What _____?　

**a** I like to act.

　I _____ an actor.

**b** I like to cook.

　I _____ to be a chef.

**c** I like to dance.

　I _____.

**d** I like animals.

　I _____.

**10** **Look and write.**

**1**

_____?

She wants to be a dancer.

**2**

_____?

He wants to be a teacher.

**3**

_____?

She wants to be a doctor.

**4**

_____?

He wants to be an athlete.

　　　　　How did I do?　☆ ☆ ☆

## 11  Look and write.

**1** What does she want to be?

_____

**3** What does she want to be?

_____

**2** What does he want to be?

_____

**4** What does he want to be?

_____

## 12  Read and match. Then write.  | to cook    to run |

**1** What does he want
   to be?

**2** What does she want
   to be?

**a** She wants to be a chef.
   She likes _____.

**b** He wants to be an athlete.
   He likes _____.

**13** **Look and write.**

| farmer | hairdresser | server |

1 _____   2 _____   3 _____

 **14** **Read and write. Then listen and check.**

104

| cut | grows | makes | sells | takes |

Goods are products. People produce goods: a farmer
¹ _____ food, and a carpenter ² _____ a table.
People also buy and sell goods. Food, books, clothes, and houses
are goods.

Some people don't produce goods. They provide services.
Hairdressers ³ _____ your hair. Nurses take care of you.
These are services.

A restaurant provides goods and services. It ⁵ _____
goods – food and drink. It also provides a service when the
server ⁶ _____ the food to the tables.

**How did I do?** ☆☆☆

**15** **Find and circle** **ar**, **er**, **and** **or**.

e    ur    or    r

a    er    ee    o

ar    ir    i    ae

**16** **Read and circle** **ar**, **er**, **and** **or**.

**1** arm **2** corn **3** teacher **4** car

**17** **Match the words with the same sounds.**

**1** singer **a** for

**2** born **b** art

**3** cart **c** letter

**110**
**18** **Listen and write** **ar**, **er**, **and** **or**. **Then chant.**

I want to be a ¹sing _____

² _____ an artist painting ³ _____ t.

I want to be a ⁴teach _____

Or a farmer with a ⁵c _____ t!

**How did I do?** ☆ ☆ ☆

### 19 Look, write, and match.

1 I like art.

**a**

I want to be a

_____.

2 I like science.

**b**

I want to be an

_____.

3 I like math.

**c**

I want to be a

_____.

4 I like music.

**d**

I want to be a

_____.

### 20 Find and write the sentences.

1 `math.` `I` `like` _____

2 `I` `be` `to` `a` `want` `teacher.` _____

3 `I` `art.` `like` _____

4 `writer.` `want` `a` `to` `be` `I` _____

**How did I do?** ☆ ☆ ☆

**21** **Look and write. What do they want to be?**

actor     artist     chef     dancer     teacher     vet

ACROSS ➜   3    5   6

DOWN ⬇

1

2

4

**22** **Write. What do you want to be? Why?**

_____

_____

# 6 My Day

**114**

### 1 Listen and ✓. Then write.

**1**  **a**   **b**     **2**  **a**   **b**

☐ ☐ ☐ ☐

_____    _____

**3**  **a**   **b**     **4**  **a**   **b**

☐ ☐ ☐ ☐

_____    _____

### 2 Read, draw, and say.

**1**

one o'clock

**2**

ten o'clock

How did I do?   ☆ ☆ ☆

# Song

**3** **Listen and sing. Look at the pictures. Then number in order.**

118

a

## What Time Is It?

b

Tick, tock. It's seven o'clock.
Time to **get up** and get dressed.
I want to stay in bed,
But it's time to brush my teeth!

Tick, tock. It's eight o'clock.
At nine o'clock, I **start school**.
I eat my breakfast and get my books.
I love school, it's cool!

c

Tick, tock. It's three o'clock.
There's no more school today.
I do my homework, and I **go out**.
And there's my friend to play.

d

Now it's evening, and it's eight o'clock,
And it's time to **go to bed**.
I watch TV and read my book.
Time to sleep now, good night!

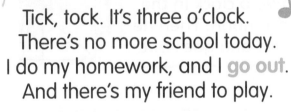

## 4 Look at 3. Write.

**1** I get up at _____.

**2** I start school at _____.

**3** I go out at _____.

**4** I go to bed at _____.

.......................................................................................

**How did I do?** ☆☆☆

Unit 6 **55**

**5** **Read. Then write in order.**

## Max's Day

Max gets up at two o'clock in the afternoon. Then he eats and goes out.

When does Max come back?

He comes back at seven o'clock, then he sleeps again.

1 _____

2 _____

3 _____

4 _____

5 _____

Max comes home.

Max eats.

Max gets up.

Max goes out.

Max sleeps again.

**THINK BIG**

How many hours do I sleep?
I go to bed at _____ in the evening.
I get up at _____ in the morning.
I sleep for _____ hours.

**How did I do?** ☆ ☆ ☆

**122**

**6** **Listen and write.**

1 get up: 7:00   2 start school:

3 finish school:   4 go out:

5 watch TV:   6 go to bed:

**7** **Look at 6. Write.**

1 When do you get up?
2 When do you start school?
3 When do you finish school?
4 When do you go out?
5 When do you watch TV?
6 When do you go to bed?

I get up _at seven o'clock_____.
I start school at _____.
I finish school at _____.
I do homework at _____.
I eat dinner at _____.
I go to bed at _____.

**How did I do?** ☆ ☆ ☆

| | |
|---|---|
| When **does** he/she **get up**? | He/She **gets up** at 6:00. |
| When **do** you/they **go to** bed? | I/They **go to** bed at 8:00. |
| When **does** the movie **start**? | It **starts** at 7:00. |

**8** **Read and circle. Then draw and write the time.**

**1** When **do** / **does** she play soccer?

She **play** / **plays** soccer at 4:00.

4:00

**2** When **do** / **does** he watch TV?

He **watch** / **watches** TV at 5:00.

_____

**3** When **do** / **does** you eat lunch?

I **eat** / **eats** lunch at 1:00.

_____

**4** When **do** / **does** they get up?

They **get** / **gets** up at 7:00.

_____

**5** When **do** / **does** the bus come?

The bus **come** / **comes** at 10:00.

_____

**How did I do?** ☆ ☆ ☆

**9** **Write about you. Add the times.**

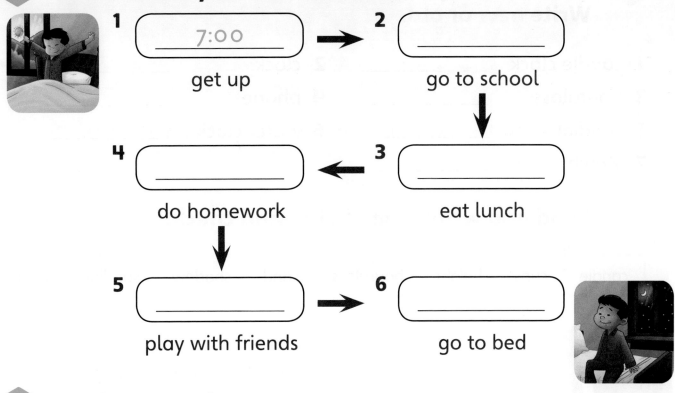

1  _____7:00_____  →  2  _____

get up                        go to school

4  _____  ←  3  _____

do homework                    eat lunch

5  _____  →  6  _____

play with friends              go to bed

**10** **Look at 9. Write.**

**1** When do you get up?

   I get up at 7:00.

**2** When do you go to school?

   _____

**3** When do you do eat lunch?

   _____

**4** When do you do homework?

   _____

**5** When do you play with friends?

   _____

**6** When do you go to bed?

   _____

**11** **Are these ways to tell the time new or old?**
**Write new or old.**

**1** candle clock _____     **2** clock       _____

**3** hourglass      _____     **4** phone       _____

**5** sundial        _____     **6** water clock _____

**7** watch          _____

124
**12** **Read and write. Then listen and check.**

| candle | cups | height | hourglass | sand | shadow | sundial | water |
|--------|------|--------|-----------|------|--------|---------|-------|

This is a ¹_____ clock. When it burns, it gets shorter. The ²_____ of the candle tells you the time. You can use this clock in the day and the night.

An ³_____ uses sand to tell the time.
The ⁴_____ falls from the top to the bottom.

A ⁵_____ clock uses water to tell the time.
It works like an hourglass. It has two ⁶_____ .
The water falls from one cup to the other.

A ⁷_____ uses the sun to tell the time.
The sun makes a shadow on the sundial. The
⁸_____ tells the time.

**How did I do?** ☆ ☆ ☆

**13** **Find and circle ch, tch, and sh.**

# c   ss   th   sh

# t   k   ch   h

# tch   s   tt   sc

**14** **Read and circle ch, tch, and sh.**

**1** | ship |   **2** | chin |   **3** | witch |   **4** | fish |   **5** | rich |

**15** **Match the words with the same sounds.**

**1** match            **a** shop

**2** chip             **b** watch

**3** dish             **c** lunch

**16** **Listen and write ch, tch, and sh. Then chant.**

130

Watch the ¹wi____,

She's having ²lun____!

Fries and ³fi____

From a ⁴di____!

Fishy Corner

**17** **School starts at 8:00. Help Anna get to school on time. Follow the paths and choose 😊 or 😕.**

**a**

She gets up at six o'clock.

She eats breakfast at seven o'clock.

She gets to school at eight o'clock.

**b**

She gets her backpack ready the night before school.

She brushes her teeth at nine o'clock.

She gets to school at ten o'clock.

**18** **How do you get to school on time? Check (✓) and draw one step.**

- [ ] I get up early on school days.
- [ ] I get dressed quickly and eat breakfast.
- [ ] I get my backpack ready the night before school.
- [ ] I always get to school on time.

**How did I do?** ☆ ☆ ☆

**19** **Write the words. Then color the times.**

> brushes – **green**   finishes – **brown**   o'clock – **orange**
> school – **blue**      six – **purple**       homework – **red**

**1** I start _____ at nine o'clock.

**2** He _____ his teeth at eight o'clock.

**3** The movie _____ at five o'clock.

**4** I do my _____ at four o'clock.

**5** She reads a book at seven _____.

**6** They eat chicken and salad at _____ o'clock.

**20** **Look and learn.**

**1** When _____ they eat lunch?

They _____ lunch at _____.

**2** When _____ she brush her teeth?

She _____ her teeth at _____.

**3** When _____ he go to bed?

He _____ to bed at _____.

**1** **Look, find, and number.**

**MY TOWN**

**1** bus stop
**2** computer store
**3** supermarket

**2** **Mark is visiting a small town. What can he do? Look at the town and ✓.**

### Mark's To-do List

☐ buy a book          ☐ mail a letter
☐ go to a restaurant  ☐ buy fruit
                      ☐ watch a movie

**3** **Think and draw. In the town, there isn't a _____.**

**4** **Use the list in 2. Write a paragraph about Mark's day. Write a title.**

## DREAM JOBS

4 artist
5 doctor
6 athlete

## MY DAY

7 brush teeth
8 get up
9 go to bed

# 7 My Favorite Food

## Vocabulary

**1** **Look and match.**

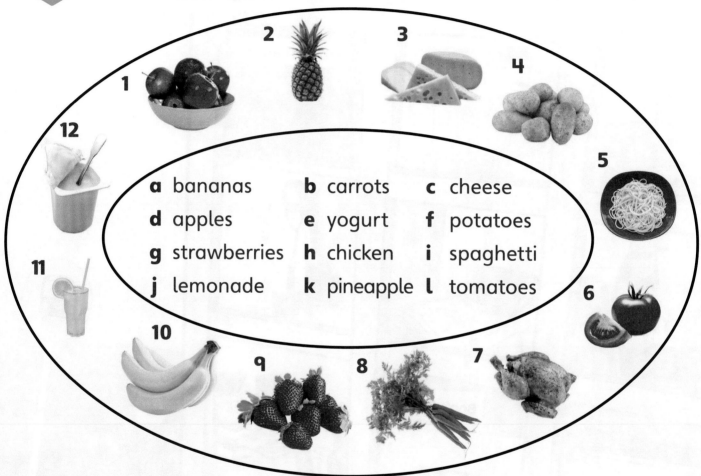

| | | |
|---|---|---|
| **a** bananas | **b** carrots | **c** cheese |
| **d** apples | **e** yogurt | **f** potatoes |
| **g** strawberries | **h** chicken | **i** spaghetti |
| **j** lemonade | **k** pineapple | **l** tomatoes |

**2** **Look and write.**

I like _____ and _____. I don't like _____.

How did I do? ☆☆☆

**138**

**3** **Listen and sing. Match and write.**

b

d

f

## Let's Eat Lunch!

It's twelve o'clock.
Let's eat lunch!
I have some bananas.
We can eat a bunch!

Do you like tomatoes?
I like tomatoes. I really do.
What about potatoes?
I like potatoes, too. Do you?

Carrots and corn,
Chicken and cheese,
I like them all.
Can I have more, please?

Have some lemonade
And a sandwich, too.
You and I can share some pie.
I like eating lunch with you.

**4** **Write and draw.**

What do you want?

I want _____.

**5**  **Read. Then circle T for true or F for false.**

## Do You Like Fruit?

It's four o'clock, boys. Do you want a snack?

Yes, please, Dad.

But I don't like bananas.

Jamie doesn't like bananas, either.

Do you like pineapple?

Yes, I do. I like pineapple.

**1** It's six o'clock.  **T**  **F**

**2** Dan and Jamie want a snack.  **T**  **F**

**3** Dan likes bananas.  **T**  **F**

**4** Jamie doesn't like bananas.  **T**  **F**

**5** Dan likes pineapple.  **T**  **F**

**THINK BIG**

**Circle the fruit.**

carrots        chicken        bananas

oranges                apples

potatoes        yogurt

How did I do?  ☆ ☆ ☆

### 6  What do you like? Listen and circle.

**1** a   b

**2** a   b

**3** a   b

### 7  Look and write.

**1**

I like _____

_____.

I don't like _____.

**2**

I like _____.

I don't like _____

_____.

**3**

I like _____

_____.

I don't like _____.

**4**

I like _____.

I don't like _____

_____.

# Grammar

| | |
|---|---|
| **Do** you **like** fruit? | Yes, I **do**. I like apples and bananas.<br>No, I **don't**. I like cheese. |
| **Do** they **like** vegetables? | Yes, they **do**. They like carrots and potatoes.<br>No, they **don't**. They like fruit. |
| **Does** he/she **like** fruit? | Yes, he/she **does**. He/She likes pineapple and strawberries.<br>No, he/she **doesn't**. He/She likes yogurt. |

**8**  **Look and circle.**

**1**

**Do / Does** she like strawberries?

Yes, she **do / does**.

**2**

**Do / Does** he like tomatoes?

No, he **don't / doesn't**.

**3**

**Do / Does** they like corn?

Yes, they **do / does**.

**9**  **Match. Then write.**

**1**  Do you like chicken?

**a** 😊 Yes, he _____.

**2**  Do they like tomatoes?

**b** ☹ No, I _____.

**3**  Does he like yogurt?

**c** 😊 😊 Yes, they _____.

**How did I do?** ☆ ☆ ☆

**10** **Look and write.**

| | 🥕 | 🥔 | 🍗 | 🥛 |
|---|---|---|---|---|
| Suki | 😊 | 😊 | 😖 | 😊 |
| Ruben | 😖 | 😊 | 😖 | 😊 |
| Mary | 😊 | 😖 | 😊 | 😊 |
| You | ⚪ | ⚪ | ⚪ | ⚪ |

😊 = like

😖 = doesn't like

**1** _____Does_____ Suki _____like_____ carrots? _____Yes, she does_____.

**2** _____ Ruben _____ chicken? _____.

**3** _____ Mary _____ potatoes? _____.

**4** _____ Mary and Ruben _____ yogurt?

_____.

**5** _____ you _____ yogurt? _____.

**11** **Read and circle. Then answer for you.**

**1** Does your **mom / friend / brother** like vegetables?

_____

**2** Do your **parents / friends / brothers** like fruit?

_____

**3** Does your **dad / friend / sister** like spaghetti?

_____

**How did I do?** ⭐ ⭐ ⭐

**12** **Are the snacks healthy or unhealthy? Put a ✓ or a ✗.**

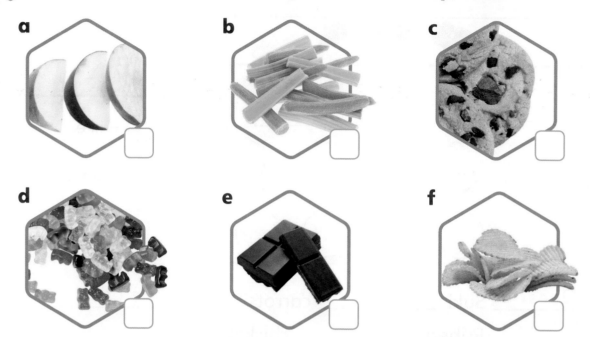

a

b

c

d

e

f

**13** **Read and write. Then listen and check.**

144

| healthy | labels | salt | sugar | unhealthy |

Some foods are healthy and good for our body. Some snacks are ¹_____ because they have too much sugar, fat, or salt in them.

²_____ in cookies and candy makes us fatter and is bad for our teeth.

Too much fat also makes us fatter. Too much fat and salt is bad for our heart. Chocolate has a lot of fat in it, and chips have a lot of ³_____ in them.

Always read the ⁴_____ on snacks and choose only ⁵_____ snacks.

**How did I do?** ☆ ☆ ☆

**14**  **Find and circle ee and ie.**

e    ai    i    ie

ey    a    ee    ea

oi    ar    u    ei

**15**  **Read and circle ee and ie.**

**1** | bee |   **2** | tie |   **3** | sheep |   **4** | pie |

**16**  **Match the words with the same sounds.**

**1** lie                    **a** feet

**2** see                   **b** cried

**17**  **Listen and write the words. Then chant.**

150

"¹_____ the ²_____!"

³_____ the ⁴_____.

"⁵_____ the ⁶_____!"

⁷_____ the ⁸_____.

**18** **Look and circle.**

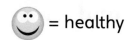 = healthy

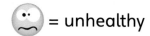 = unhealthy

1

salad

2

chips

3

cookies

4

carrots

5

chocolate

6

apples

**19** **Find and write the sentences.**

1 | one | Just | please. | cookie,

_____

2 | thanks. | No | me, | chips | for

_____

**How did I do?** ☆ ☆ ☆

**20**  **What do you like? Look and write five foods.**

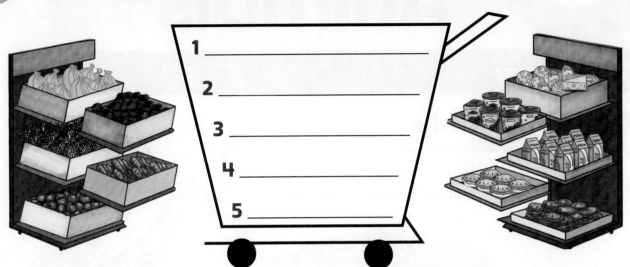

1 _____
2 _____
3 _____
4 _____
5 _____

**21**  **Look and write.**

1

Does he like bananas?
Yes, _____.

2

He _____ carrots.
He _____ cheese.

3

Does she like chicken?
No, _____.
She _____ yogurt.

4

They _____ cheese.
They _____ chicken.

# Wild Animals

## Vocabulary

**1** **Look and write.**

> cheetahs   giraffes   hippos   kangaroos
> monkeys   polar bears   zebras

ZOO

1 _____

2 _____

3 _____

4 _____

5 _____

6 _____

7 _____

**2** **Look and match.**

**1** crocodile   **2** elephant   **3** cheetah   **4** peacock

a    b    c    d

**How did I do?**   ☆ ☆ ☆

# Song

**3** **Listen and sing. Write the words.**

## To the Zoo!

I really like animals!
Do you like them, too?
That's why I'm so happy.
We're going to the zoo!

A ¹_____ can jump.
A ²_____ can jump, too.
Crocodiles can chase and swim.
And you, what can you do?

A ³_____ can't fly or jump up high.
An ⁴_____ can't climb trees.
Fish can't run, and hippos can't fly.
Come and see them.
Oh, yes, please!

Now it's time to say goodbye
To every animal here.
But we can come back
And see them every year!

kangaroo

elephant

monkey

giraffe

**4** **What animals do you like seeing at the zoo?**

_____  _____  _____

_____  _____  _____

**How did I do?** ☆☆☆

## 5 Read and circle.

## Monkeys Are Great!

1 **Monkeys / Hippos** can climb trees.

2 **Monkeys / Hippos** can eat a lot of food.

3 **Monkeys / Hippos** can jump.

4 **Monkeys / Hippos** have big mouths.

5 **Jamie / Jenny** can eat a lot.

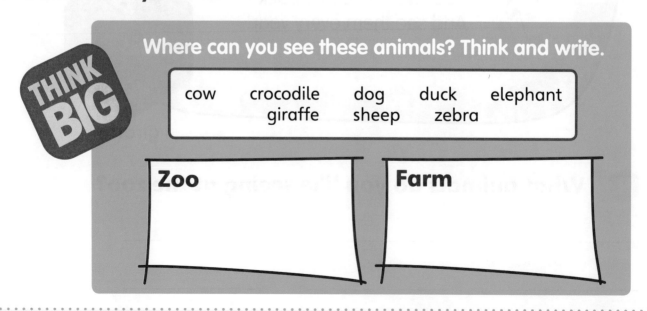

THINK BIG

**Where can you see these animals? Think and write.**

| cow | crocodile | dog | duck | elephant |
| | giraffe | sheep | zebra | |

**Zoo**

**Farm**

How did I do?

**6** **Listen. Write and match.**

| elephant | kangaroo | lion | monkey |

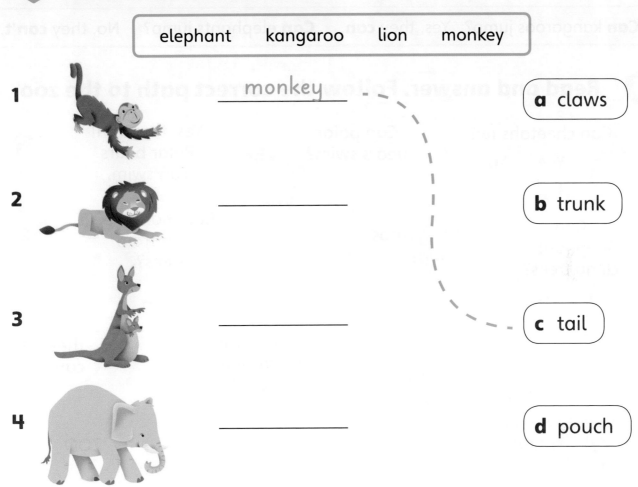

1 _monkey_      **a** claws

2 _____      **b** trunk

3 _____      **c** tail

4 _____      **d** pouch

**7** **Draw an animal. Then write answers.**

1 What is it? _____

2 Can it climb trees? _____

3 Can it fly? _____

4 Does it have a tail? _____

# Grammar

**Can** a kangaroo jump? Yes, it **can**.　**Can** an elephant jump? No, it **can't**.

**Can** kangaroos jump?　Yes, they **can**.　**Can** elephants jump?　No, they **can't**.

**8** **Read and answer. Follow the correct path to the zoo.**

**9** **Match and write. Use** can **or** can't.

1  Can a giraffe swim?

a Yes, they _____.

2  Can monkeys climb trees?

b Yes, it _____.

3  Can a cheetah chase animals?

c No, it _____.

**How did I do?** ☆ ☆ ☆

**10** **Look at the chart. Write questions and answers.**

|  | run | jump | climb trees | catch animals |
|---|---|---|---|---|
| **1** giraffes | yes | no | no | no |
| **2** polar bears | yes | yes | yes | yes |
| **3** hippos | yes | no | no | no |
| **4** cheetahs | yes | yes | yes | yes |
| **5** zebras | yes | yes | no | no |
| **6** kangaroos | no | yes | no | no |

**1** _Can giraffes_____ run?

_Yes_____, they _can_____.

**2** _____ jump?

_____, they _____.

**3** _____ climb trees?

_____, they _____.

**4** _____ catch animals?

_____, they _____.

**5** _____ run?

_____, they _____.

**6** _____ climb trees?

_____, they _____.

**How did I do?** ☆☆☆

**11  Read and write.**

1  Tigers live in the _____.

2  Fish live in the _____.

3  A lizard lives in the _____.

4  A deer lives in the _____.

desert
forest
jungle
ocean

164
**12  Listen, read, and match.**

1  It's hot, and it rains a lot. Monkeys, birds, butterflies, and tigers live here. _____

2  It's cool and dark in the forest, and there are a lot of trees. _____

3  Lizards and snakes live here. There aren't many plants because it's very dry. _____

4  The ocean covers 71% of the planet. Many kinds of fish live in the ocean. _____

**a**  About 6% of the planet is desert.

**b**  Deer, raccoons, and foxes live here, too.

**c**  Whales and seals also live in the salty water.

**d**  The jungle covers only 2% of the planet, but 50% of all plants and animals live here.

**How did I do?**  ☆☆☆

**13** **Find and circle ou and ow.**

u    a    ow    w

oo    ou    o    v

e    oe    au    uo

**14** **Read and circle ou and ow.**

1 | you    2 | owl    3 | soup    4 | cow

**15** **Match the words with the same sounds.**

1 down      a route

2 group      b town

**16** **Listen and write the words. Then chant.**

170

An ¹_____ went
²_____ to ³_____
To see a ⁴_____ of
⁵_____ drinking
⁶_____.

**17** **Look, listen, and write.**

| smart | strong | beautiful | amazing |

**1** I like peacocks.

They're so _____.

**2** Monkeys are so

_____.

**3** Giraffes are _____.
Their necks are so long.

**4** Elephants are very

_____.

**18** **Find and write the describing words.**

1 _____ z a a m n g i
2 _____ a m s t r
3 _____ f l u t i u e b a
4 _____ o g n t s r

How did I do? ☆ ☆ ☆

**19** **Look and write.**

ACROSS ➡

3   5   6

DOWN ⬇

1   2   4

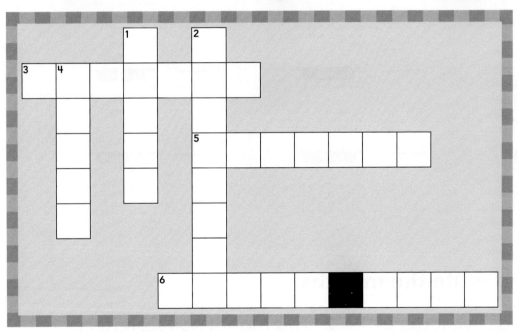

**20** **Write. Then match the questions with the answers.**

1 _____ a monkey climb trees?   **a** No, they _____.

2 _____ parrots fly?   **b** Yes, it _____.

3 _____ a peacock swim?   **c** Yes, they _____.

4 _____ snakes run?   **d** No, it _____.

# 9 Fun All Year

## Vocabulary

**1** **Number the months in order.**

| April | January | May |
| --- | --- | --- |
| August | July | November |
| December | June | October |
| February | March | September |

**2** **Read and write the months.**

**1** This month has five letters.
This month is before April.

_____

**2** This month has six letters.
This month is after July.

_____

**3** This month has eight letters.
This month is between
October and December.

_____

How did I do? ☆ ☆ ☆

### 178
**3** **Listen and sing. Then write.**

# I Like July!

¹_____ is my favorite month.
I like ²_____, too.
I'm happy and on vacation,
There is so much to do!

I also like ³_____.
That's when I start school.
I'm so excited, aren't you?
My friends will be there, too!

I don't like ⁴_____.
It's very, very cold.
But then it is my birthday, too.
This year, I'm eight years old!

August

July

December

September

**4** **What month do you like? Write. Then circle how many days it has.**

_____

| S | M | T | W | T | F | S |
|---|---|---|---|---|---|---|
|  |  | 1 | 2 | 3 | 4 | 5 |
| 6 | 7 | 8 | 9 | 10 | 11 | 12 |
| 13 | 14 | 15 | 16 | 17 | 18 | 19 |
| 20 | 21 | 22 | 23 | 24 | 25 | 26 |
| 27 | 28 | 29 | 30 | 31 |  |  |

**How did I do?** ☆☆☆

## 5 Read and write.

# Fun in August!

**1** Jenny's favorite month is

_____.

**2** Jenny _____ goes on

vacation in December.

**3** Dan _____ goes on

vacation in the winter.

**4** It's too _____ in the

winter.

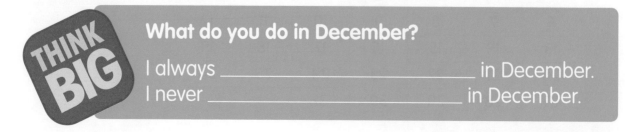

**THINK BIG**

**What do you do in December?**

I always _____ in December.

I never _____ in December.

How did I do?  ☆ ☆ ☆

**182**

**6**  **Listen. Then circle and match.**

**1** Mother's Day is in **May / March**.
Mom wants to go to
**the park / the beach**.

**2** Father's Day is in **June / July**.
Dad always goes to a
**baseball / basketball** game.

**3** Children's Day is in
**October / November**.
They want to visit their
**cousins / friends**.

**4** Grandparents' Day is in
**September / December**.
Grandma wants to
**skateboard / see a movie**.

**5** Molly's birthday is in
**January / June**.
She always **has a party /
eats cookies**.

**a**

**b**

**c**

**d**

**e**

**How did I do?** ☆☆☆

| What does he/she do in January? | He/She **always** has a New Year's party in January. |
|---|---|
| What do they do in the spring? | They **always** play baseball in the park. |
| Do you go on vacation in the winter? | No, I/we don't. I/We **never** go on vacation in the winter. |

**7** **Look at the calendar. Then read and circle.**

**1** Do they have a New Year's party in June?

No, they **always** / **never** have a New Year's party in June.

**2** What do they do in June?

They **always** / **never** visit their cousins in June.

**3** What do they celebrate in June?

They **always** / **never** celebrate Father's Day in June.

**4** Do they have Billy's birthday party in June?

No, they **always** / **never** have his birthday party in June.

It isn't Billy's birthday.

## June

| Sun | Mon | Tues | Wed | Thur | Fri | Sat |
|---|---|---|---|---|---|---|
|  |  |  |  | 1 | 2 | 3 |
| 4 | 5 | 6 | 7 | 8 | 9 | Visit Cousins 10 |
| 11 | 12 | 13 | 14 | Sally's Birthday 15 | 16 | 17 |
| Father's Day 18 | 19 | 20 | 21 | 22 | 23 | Beach 24 |
| 25 | 26 | 27 | 28 | 29 | 30 |  |

**8** **Answer about you. Write and circle.**

Do you go on vacation in June?

_____, I _____. I **always** / **never** go on vacation in June.

How did I do? ☆ ☆ ☆

**9** **Look and write always or never.**

Hi, I'm Julia. I always skate on ice in the winter.

|  | winter | spring | summer | fall |
|---|---|---|---|---|
| **always** | skate on ice | have a party | swim | visit my cousins |
| **never** | ride my bike | go on vacation | go to school | celebrate New Year's |

**1** What does she do in the winter?
She _____ rides her bike. She _____ skates on ice.

**2** What does she do in the spring?
She _____ has a party.
She _____ goes on vacation.

**3** What does she do in the summer?
She _____ swims. She _____ goes to school.

**4** What does she do in the fall?
She _____ celebrates New Year's. She _____ visits her cousins.

**10** **Choose a season. Then answer about you.**

What do you do in the _____?
I always _____. I never _____.

**11** **Read and match for you.**

In my country,

1 December and January are       **a** in the spring.

2 April and May are              **b** in the summer.

3 July and August are            **c** in the fall.

4 September and October are      **d** in the winter.

**12** **Listen, circle, and match.**
184

**a**

1  On May Day, children in England hold **wishes / ribbons** and dance around a **tree / pole**.

**b**

2  In February and March, there are carnivals in Italy. People wear masks and throw small pieces of paper called **bamboo / confetti**.

**c**

3  The Mid-Autumn Festival in China happens when the **star / moon** is very big. Children wear **ribbons / costumes** and eat mooncakes.

**d**

4  In the summer, people in Japan celebrate Tanabata, the star festival. They **hang / wear** wishes on a bamboo **ribbon / wish** tree.

**13** **Write the alphabet in the correct order.**

Aa | __ | __ | __d | __ | F_ | __ | __h | I__

Q__ | __ | O_ | __ | M_ | __ | __k | __

__ | __t | __ | V_ | __ | __x | Y_ | __

**14** **Listen and write the letters and words. Then chant.**

A, B, C, ¹____, E, ²____, G.

I can see an ant and a ³_____.
What can you see?

H, I, ⁴____, K, L, ⁵____, N, O, ⁶____.

I can see a ⁷_____ and some ink. What can you see?

Q, ⁸____, S, T, ⁹____, V.

I can see a ¹⁰_____ and a snake.
What can you ¹¹_____?

W, ¹²____, Y, and ¹³____.

¹⁴_____ yellow wolves and
a ¹⁵_____ are what I see!

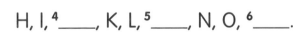

**How did I do?** ☆ ☆ ☆

**15** **Read, look, and match.**

**1** In the spring, he rides his bike.

**a**

**b**

**2** In the summer, she likes to swim.

**c**

**3** In the fall, they rake leaves.

**d**

**4** In the winter, they skate on ice.

**16** **Find and write the words. Then match each season with the months in your country.**

**1** t n r e w i _____

**2** r p s g n i _____

**3** l a f l _____

**4** m r e u s m _____

**a** December, January, February

**b** March, April, May

**c** June, July, August

**d** September, October, November

**How did I do?** ☆ ☆ ☆

**17** **Complete the dialog.**

| always | Do | don't |
|--------|----|----|
| never | What | |

**Maria:** ¹_____ do you do in the winter?

**Peter:** We ²_____ skate on ice.

**Maria:** We always visit our cousins in the winter.
We ³_____ skate on ice.

**Peter:** ⁴_____ you swim at the beach in the summer?

**Maria:** No, we don't. We ⁵_____ swim at the beach in the summer. We always go to the swimming pool and eat ice cream!

**18** **Draw and write about you.**

**1** What do you always do in the fall?

_____
_____
_____

**2** What do you never do in the spring?

_____
_____
_____

## 1 Look, find, and number.

**2** **Look at 1 and write. Add one food word, one animal word, and one month word.**

**3** **Look at the table, think, and circle one food in red:**

What do you like to eat for lunch?

**4** **Look at the table, think, and circle one food in blue:**

What do you never eat for lunch?

**5** **Look, think, and circle in green.**

There's a hat on an elephant. That's silly. What other silly things can you see?

**6** **In Your Classroom**

Work in groups and share.

### FOOD

> **1** carrots
>
> **2** cheese
>
> **3** bananas
>
> _____

# 🔍 ANIMALS

**4** zebra
**5** elephant
**6** giraffe
_____

# 🔍 MONTHS

**7** summer month
**8** winter month
**9** fall month
_____

| What**'s** he/she **doing**? | He**'s**/She**'s reading** a book. |
| What **are** they **doing**? | They**'re gluing** pictures. |

**1** **Circle the correct form of the verb. Then match.**

**1** What **is / are** he doing?    **a** She's coloring.

**2** What **is / are** they doing?    **b** They're watching a movie.

**3** What **is / are** she doing?    **c** He's counting.

| How many pictures are there? | **There's** one picture. |
| How many books are there? | **There are** three books. |

**2** **Look and write. Use There's or There are.**

**1** _____ one teacher.

**2** _____ one book.

**3** _____ nine students.

     **How did I do?** ☆ ☆ ☆

| | |
|---|---|
| What **does** he/she **like to do**? | He/She **likes to skate**. |
| What **do** they **like to do**? | They **like to play basketball**. |

**1** **Read and circle.**

**1** What **do / does** he like to do?

He **like / likes** to play basketball.

**2** What **do / does** they like to do?

They **like / likes** to play hide-and-seek.

**3** What **do / does** she like to do?

She **like / likes** to jump.

**2** **Look and write the question. Then write the answer.**

| listen   use |
|---|

**1**

What _____ doing?

He _____ the computer.

**2**

What _____ doing?

They _____

to music.

# Extra Grammar Practice

| Where's the TV? | It's on the table. |
|---|---|
| Where **are** the chairs? | **They're** in the living room. |

**1** **Look and write Where's or Where are.**

**1** _____ the keys?     **2** _____ the phone?

**3** _____ the soccer ball?     **4** _____ the skates?

**2** **Look at 1. Answer the questions.**

**1** _____ in the bedroom.     **2** _____ on the bed.

**3** _____ in the bathtub.     **4** _____ next to the chair.

| My mom's phone is on the dresser. | Ben's keys are on the table. |
|---|---|

**3** **Read and circle.**

**1** Where are **Mom / Mom's** keys?

**2** My **cousins / cousin's** are riding their bikes.

**3** **Emily / Emily's** bedroom is next to the bathroom.

**4** **Joes / Joe's** clothes are in the closet.

    **How did I do?** ☆ ☆ ☆

> I/We/They/You **want to** mail a letter.    He/She **wants to** go to the park.

**1  Read and circle.**

**1** I **want** / **wants** to buy a book.

**2** My aunt and uncle **want** / **wants** to go to the computer store.

**3** Julia **want** / **wants** to mail a letter.

**4** He **want** / **wants** to eat.

| **Is there** a post office near here? | Yes, **there is**. |
| --- | --- |
| **Is there** a bank on Elm Street? | No, **there isn't**. |

**2  Look and write.**

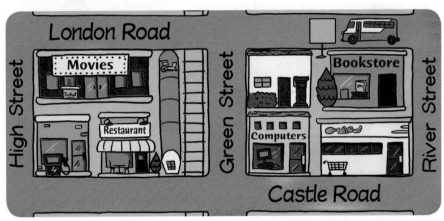

**1 A:** Is there a bookstore on High Street?

**B:** _____

**2 A:** Is there a computer store on River Street?

**B:** _____

**3 A:** _____ a movie theater near the train station?

**B:** _____

**4 A:** Let's eat.

_____ a restaurant near here?

**B:** Yes, _____.

**How did I do?**  ☆ ☆ ☆

# Extra Grammar Practice

| | |
|---|---|
| What **do** you **want to be**? | I **want to be** an actor. |
| What **does** he/she **want to be**? | He/She **wants to be** a doctor. |

**1** **Look and write.**

**1**

What does he want to be?

He _____.

**2**

What does she want to be?

She _____.

**3**

_____?

She wants to be a pilot.

**4**

_____?

He wants to be a chef.

**5**

_____?

He _____.

**6**

What do you want to be?

_____

**How did I do?**  ☆ ☆ ☆

| | |
|---|---|
| When **does** he/she **get up**? | He/She **gets up** at 6:00. |
| When **do** you/they **go to** bed? | I/They **go to** bed at 8:00. |
| When **does** the movie **start**? | It **starts** at 7:00. |

**1** **Look and match. Then write the questions and answers.**

**1** When

**2** When

they go to school?

do     she get up?

does    she go to bed?

he finish school?

**3** When

**4** When

1 _____?

_____

2 _____?

_____

3 _____?

_____

4 _____?

_____

| | |
|---|---|
| **Do** you **like** fruit? | Yes, I **do**. I like apples and bananas.<br>No, I **don't**. I like cheese. |
| **Do** they **like** vegetables? | Yes, they **do**. They like carrots and potatoes.<br>No, they **don't**. They like fruit. |
| **Does** he/she **like** fruit? | Yes, he/she **does**. He/She likes pineapple and strawberries.<br>No, he/she **doesn't**. He/She likes yogurt. |

**1** **Read and circle.**

1 **Do / Does** she like chicken? No, she **don't / doesn't**.
She likes sandwiches.

2 **Do / Does** they like snacks? Yes, they **do / does**.

3 **Do / Does** she like cheese? Yes, she **do / does**.

4 **Do / Does** they like tomatoes? No, they **don't / doesn't**.
They like potatoes.

5 **Do / Does** you like strawberries? Yes, I **do / does**.
I love strawberries!

**2** **Look and write the questions and answers.**

| 1 you | bananas | :( |
| 2 Emma | apples | :( |
| 3 Sue and Hugo | carrots | :) |

1 _____ you _____ bananas?  _____

2 _____ she _____ apples?  _____

3 _____ they _____ carrots?  _____

**How did I do?**  ☆☆☆

# Extra Grammar Practice

| | |
|---|---|
| **Can** a kangaroo jump? Yes, it **can**. | **Can** an elephant jump? No, it **can't**. |
| **Can** kangaroos jump?  Yes, they **can**. | **Can** elephants jump?  No, they **can't**. |

**1** **Read. Circle T for true or F for false.**

**1** Cheetahs can run.      T     F

**2** A giraffe can fly.      T     F

**3** A polar bear can jump.      T     F

**4** An elephant can talk.      T     F

**5** Hippos can climb trees.      T     F

**6** Kangaroos can swim.      T     F

**2** **Look at 1. Correct the false sentences. Use can't.**

**1** _____

**2** _____

**3** _____

**4** _____

**3** **Write the questions. Use the words in the box.
Then write the answers.**

> chase   fly   talk   write

**1** Can a cheetah _____ a zebra?     Yes, _____.

**2** _____ a cheetah _____?     No, _____.

**3** _____ cheetahs _____?     No, _____.

**4** _____ cheetahs _____ their name?     No, _____.

**How did I do?** ☆ ☆ ☆

| What does he/she do in January? | He/She **always** has a New Year's party in January. |
| What do they do in the spring? | They **always** play basketball in the park. |
| Do you go on vacation in the winter? | No, I/we don't. I/We **never** go on vacation in the winter. |

**1** **Read and circle. Answer about you.**

**1** Do you start school in September?

**Yes / No**. I **always** / **never** start school in September.

**2** Does your father like to read books?

**Yes / No**. He **always** / **never** reads books.

**3** Do you like to swim in the winter?

**Yes / No**. I **always** / **never** swim in the winter.

**4** Does your family go on vacation in the fall?

**Yes / No**. We **always** / **never** go on vacation in the fall.

**5** Does your mom celebrate her birthday in the spring?

**Yes / No**. She **always** / **never** celebrates her birthday in the spring.

**2** **Look at the calendar. Write** always **or** never.

**Anna:** What does he do in January?
**Bill:** He ¹_____ celebrates New Year's Day.
**Anna:** Does he celebrate the New Year in February, too?
**Bill:** No. He ²_____ celebrates the New Year in February! That's silly.

### January

| | Sun | Mon | Tues | Wed | Thu | Fri | Sat |
| --- | --- | --- | --- | --- | --- | --- | --- |
| | 1 New Year's Day | 2 | 3 | 4 | 5 | 6 | 7 |
| | 8 | 9 | 10 | 11 | 12 | 13 | 14 |
| | 15 | 16 | 17 | 18 | 19 | 20 | 21 |
| | 22 | 23 | 24 | 25 | 26 | 27 | 28 |
| | 29 | 30 | 31 | | | | |

**How did I do?**

**Pearson Education Limited**

KAO Two
KAO ParkHarlow
Essex
CM17 9NA
England
and Associated Companies throughout the world.

English.com/BigEnglish2

© Pearson Education Limited 2017

Authorised adaptation from the United States edition entitled Big English, 1st Edition, by Mario Herrera and Christopher Sol Cruz. Published by Pearson Education Inc. © 2013 by Pearson Education, Inc.

The right of Mario Herrera and Christopher Sol Cruz to be identified as the authors of this Work have been asserted by them in accordance with the Copyright, Designs and Patents Act 1988.

First published 2017
Fifteenth impression 2023

ISBN: 978-1-2922-3325-3
Set in Heinemann Roman
Printed in Slovakia by Neografia

**Acknowledgements**

**Picture Credits**

The publisher would like to thank the following for their kind permission to reproduce their photographs:

(Key: b-bottom; c-centre; l-left; r-right; t-top)

**123RF.com:** 14l, captblack76 92b, Jacek Chabraszewski 21cr (top), Foresterforest 13bl, 21tl, iakov 40cl, 43b, Saidin B Jusoh 82tl, maxaltamor 28tc, Marco Mayer 75bl, Boris Ryzhkov 74tl, Wavebreak Media Ltd 3bl, Cathy Yeulet 7/1; **Alamy Stock Photo:** ableimages 55br, 103bl, Aflo Co. Ltd. 92tc, Age Fotostock / David Kennedy 89b, ARGO Images 40/3, Asia Images Group Pte Ltd 80tl, Blend Images 44tl, Cultura RM 21tr, F1online digitale Bildagentur GmbH 42t, Glow Asia RF 102r/3, Hemis 40bl, Horizon International Images Limited 60tl, Interfoto 60bl, Jurgen Magg 16 (b), 99cr, Mark Bolton Photography 92bc, Bob Masters 28tl, myLAM 92t, Graham Oliver 34 (e), Pawel Libera Images 28br, Radius Images 40/2, 43t, Uwe Umstatter 75bc, VStock 5t, 7/2, Zak Waters 52t, Gari Wyn Williams 40/4; **BananaStock:** 13cr, 21cl (bottom); **Datacraft Co Ltd:** 42b; **Fotolia.com:** apops 50c, aussieanouk 84tr, Sergiy Bykhunenko 12bl, dasharosato 40cr, f9photos 60tr, goodluz 44bl, igorphoto50 66/11, Ilike 3br, 6/5, 98tl, Michael Ireland 20 (c), Jakub Krechowicz 66/4, 67cr, 69br, krsmanovic 34 (b), Lucky Dragon 20 (b), Monkey Business 20 (d), moodboard 94 (a), motorlka 66/8, 67bl, 69bl, 74bl, Natika 72br, Tyler Olson 44cl, 48bc, 53/6, picsfive 72bc, pololia 12tr, r-o-x-o-r 40br, RT Images 27tr, 28bl, RusGri 74tc, shutswis 28tr, snaptitude 102r/2, sumnersgraphicsinc 14c, sveta 27tl, tropper2000 74bc, Tom Wang 102r/1, Monika Wisniewska 52b, yanlev 12tl, 21cr (bottom), yunuskoc 7/3; **Getty Images:** Paul Bradbury 16 (d), Diane Collins and Jordan Hollender 5b, 98tc, fotostorm 89c, Fuse 94 (d), Mike Kemp 89t, Katy McDonnell 3tr, 6/2, Juan Silva 30c, Damir Spanic 44c (right), 48tc, 53/3, Linda Steward 34 (a); **Pearson Education Ltd:** Studio 8 80br, Trevor Clifford 47l/2, 47r/3, 102l/3, Naki Kouyioumtzis 34 (c), Debbie Rowe 40/1, Jules Selmes 3tl, 6/4, 48t, 53/4, 102r/4; **Shutterstock.com:** Andresr 14r, Andrjuss 66/3, 67tl, Andy Dean Photography 44c (left), Apples Eyes Studio 52bc, Bernatets Photo 89bc, Nick Berrisford 82bl, Dean Bertoncelj 50l, Andre Blais 12br, 20 (a), 21bl, Mark Bonham 48b, 53/1, Willyam Bradberry 82br, Diego Cervo 55bl, 103tr, cycreation 43bc, davegkugler 77b, 84bl, Julie DeGuia 13br, eurobanks 72tc, Fotokostic 7/4, Stephanie Frey 30r, Warren Goldswain 55tr, 103tl, Goodluz 50r, Skazka Grez 72tl, Shawn Hempel 84tl, Jiri Hera 72bl, Hurst Photo 89tc, IB Photography 8b, idiz 77t, irin k 8t, Christopher Jones 44tr, 53/2, Evgeny Karandaev 27cl, Serhiy Kobyakov 6/3, 98tr, Vladimir Koletic 44cr, Vitaly Korovin 66/6, 67cl, Kzenon 99c, Lucky Business 5c, Bruce MacQueen 82tr, Viktar Malyshchyts 66/10, 67tr, 69tr, Rob Marmion 12cr, 13tl, 21cl (top), 47r/1, 102l/2, mexrix 66/12, Microgen 16 (a), Monkey Business Images 17, 20/1, 20/2, 20/3, 20/4, 47l/1, 47l/3, 47r/4, 66b, 80cr, 80bl, 99cl, 102l/4, Morgan Lane Photography 6/1, Dmitry Naumov 12cl, 16 (c), 94 (c), Naypong 76cr, odze 66/9, 69cr, Presniakov Oleksandr 60br, Panco 75cr, Pavia 42c, Csaba Peterdi 94 (b), Picturepartners 75cl, Stuart G Porter 76r, 105, rickyd 76cl, riekephotos 30l, Rohit Seth 47r/2, 102l/1, Alexander Ryabintsev 43tc, S-F 18t, SergiyN 80tr, Dmitriy Shironosov 53/5, 98br, Victor Shova 76l, 77tc, Slaven 52tc, Smit 54, 56, 58, Ljupco Smokovski 69tl, Bryan Solomon 72tr, 74tr, Alex Staroseltsev 66/2, James Steidl 28bc, Michaela Stejskalova 66/5, Ronald Summers 8tc, Beth Swanson 13tr, 21br, Syda Productions 18b, Tatuasha 27cr, Leah-Anne Thompson 55tl, 103br, Krishna Utkarsh Pandit 84br, Dani Vincek 66/7, 67br, Visionsi 44br, 102b, Valentyn Volkov 8bc, Tatyana Vyc 66/1, 69cl, 74br, wavebreakmedia 99bl, Tracy Whiteside 47l/4, worldswildlifewonders 77bc, zimmytws 99tr, ZouZou 75br; **SuperStock:** Blend Images 80cl; **www.imagesource.com:** photolibrary.com 34 (d)

**Cover images:** *Front:* **Getty Images:** strmko

All other images © Pearson Education

**Illustrated by**

Robin Boyer, Zaharias Papadopoulos (Hyphen), Jose Rubio, Christos Skaltas (Hyphen), Julia Wolf and Q2A Media Services.

Every effort has been made to trace the copyright holders and we apologise in advance for any unintentional omissions. We would be pleased to insert the appropriate acknowledgement in any subsequent edition of this publication.

# Tracklist

| Class CD track number | Workbook CD track number | Unit and activity number |
|---|---|---|
| 9 | 2 | Unit 1, activity 1 |
| 13 | 3 | Unit 1, activity 3 |
| 21 | 4 | Unit 1, activity 13 |
| 27 | 5 | Unit 1, activity 17 |
| 35 | 6 | Unit 2, activity 2 |
| 39 | 7 | Unit 2, activity 7 |
| 44 | 8 | Unit 2, activity 12 |
| 50 | 9 | Unit 2, activity 16 |
| 52 | 10 | Unit 2, activity 19 |
| 58 | 11 | Unit 3, activity 3 |
| 62 | 12 | Unit 3, activity 6 |
| 64 | 13 | Unit 3, activity 11 |
| 70 | 14 | Unit 3, activity 15 |
| 72 | 15 | Unit 3, activity 16 |
| 80 | 16 | Unit 4, activity 2 |
| 84 | 17 | Unit 4, activity 5 |
| 86 | 18 | Unit 4, activity 12 |
| 92 | 19 | Unit 4, activity 16 |
| 99 | 20 | Unit 5, activity 3 |
| 104 | 21 | Unit 5, activity 14 |

| Class CD track number | Workbook CD track number | Unit and activity number |
|---|---|---|
| 110 | 22 | Unit 5, activity 18 |
| 114 | 23 | Unit 6, activity 1 |
| 118 | 24 | Unit 6, activity 3 |
| 122 | 25 | Unit 6, activity 6 |
| 124 | 26 | Unit 6, activity 12 |
| 130 | 27 | Unit 6, activity 16 |
| 138 | 28 | Unit 7, activity 3 |
| 142 | 29 | Unit 7, activity 6 |
| 144 | 30 | Unit 7, activity 13 |
| 150 | 31 | Unit 7, activity 17 |
| 157 | 32 | Unit 8, activity 3 |
| 161 | 33 | Unit 8, activity 6 |
| 164 | 34 | Unit 8, activity 12 |
| 170 | 35 | Unit 8, activity 16 |
| 172 | 36 | Unit 8, activity 17 |
| 178 | 37 | Unit 9, activity 3 |
| 182 | 38 | Unit 9, activity 6 |
| 184 | 39 | Unit 9, activity 12 |
| 188 | 40 | Unit 9, activity 14 |